"Once one has attained Enlightenment, he shall regard all elders as his parents, all contemporaries as his brothers and sisters, all children as his children."

— Eastern Proverb

This book is for our parents, our brothers and sisters, and our children. This book is for the world.

GENERATIONS

ACKNOWLEDGMENTS

"Night Games" by Martin Holroyd won Second Prize in a *Poetry Digest* national (United Kingdom) competition and, along with many other poems by Mr. Holroyd, appeared in the British 1992 anthology *New Faces.* A number of his poems have appeared in the journal *Poetry Nottingham.*

"Hoofbeats" by Richard Ball was previously published in that poet's chapbook *Last Ten from the Gulag,* Whitby: The Plowman Press, 1993.

Beecher Smith's poems "Revelation", "Little Hurts", "A Woman's Tears", and "Debbie's White Christmas" were all previously published in that poet's chapbook *The Visitation of Dionysius,* Whitby: The Plowman Press, 1989.

"Parcæ" by Vassar W. Smith was first published in *The Classical Outlook,* Volume LXX, N⁰· 2, Winter, 1993. Vassar Smith's poems "Tema con Variazioni" and "Ribbons and Evergreens..." were previously published in that poet's chapbook *The Oven–Bird Chorus, "* Palo Alto: Zapizdat Publications, 1993.

GENERATIONS

The Zapizdat World Anthology

Edited by Vassar W. Smith

Featuring the Poetry of:

MARTIN HOLROYD
R. CLEMENT WOOD
J. C. WATSON
CHARLOTTE MUSE
JIM STANDISH

and also Honored to Present Poems by

JUDITH BISHOP	AURIEL YOST
RICHARD BALL	WOJCIECH ZALEWSKI
KEVIN ARNOLD	DAVID HARR
APRIL EILER	DORA KUSHNER
LARA GULARTE	ESTHER KAMKAR
BEECHER SMITH	VASSAR W. SMITH
PETER BERARDO	ANATOLE LUBOVICH
SCOTT LOWE	CAROL HANKERMEYER

Zapizdat Publications
P. O. Box 326
Palo Alto, California 94302

First Edition

ISBN 1–880964–06–6

Library of Congress
Catalog Card Number 93–61766

ZAPIZDAT PUBLICATIONS

Editor in Chief: Vassar W. Smith

Advisory Editors:

Kate M. Ague
Kevin Arnold
Scott Lowe

COPYRIGHT NOTICE

Table of Contents

GENERATIONS

GENERATIONS

Introduction

A year after the publication of *The Clock, Desperados and Jeremy,* Zapizdat publications has now published a much larger anthology with contents no less impressive and enjoyable than those of its antecessor. The title *Generations* was chosen because so many of the poems included share the theme of intergenerational relationships, whereby so often we derive our greatest insight into both the past and the future. This is hardly the only or the requisite theme of this anthology, but it did turn out to be the most recurrent, hence the most unifying. Moreover, the selections for this volume not only embrace many more poems and several more poets, but also include voices from other parts of the United States as well as from abroad.

We are very pleased to introduce to American readers the poetry of **Martin Holroyd**, who transports the reader with his gift of song and his bold but flexible use of lyric conventions. His poems celebrating the events of life and effects of time achieve that necessary but rare balance between the personal and the collective human consciousness. His poems span a broad variety of emotions and subjects. His style is distinguished by humor without flippancy, pathos without bathos. The bittersweet punch of "Choirboys and Cowboys" and the rugged tenderness of his "Poem for Emma Jane" may leave the reader with the gratifying feeling that if Holroyd's poetic fire endures, the next century might regard this poet as highly as we now regard W. B. Yeats and Dylan Thomas.

Mid-Southern poet **R. Clement Wood** writes poems of sustained narrative power. Whether in blank verse, free verse, or rhymed couplets, he draws the reader into his spell detail by detail until one reaches the end with a sensation like the snap of a hypnotist's fingers. Wood shows particularly well the layered quality of time in a person's psyche: While physically we cannot return to the past, we are constantly reminded of it, linked to it, thrust back to it by present events. In "The Death of the Fourth–Grade Teacher" Wood succeeds strikingly well in developing and unifying the poem through metonymy.

GENERATIONS

The poems of **J. C. Watson** succeed through an intricate and incredibly harmonious association of imagery. Whether depicting the physically vital but mentally moribund daily routine of a fisherman's wife or capturing the grace of a girl on the threshold of adulthood, Watson radiates vitality with every line, insight with every poem. Her work exemplifies the distinguished quality of saying in words so much more than words alone can say.

As effectively as Watson's verse embraces human experience, the well–paced, dignified poems of **Charlotte Muse** address the natural and the cosmic. In "Poets" she aptly observes that "beauty depends on an illusion of stillness," with the implicit corollary that that stillness *is* an illusion, one which can only be captured in memory and art; in the material world motion is pervasive and change inexorable.

Those who believe a poet's mission is to hold back the night of stratification and stultification, take heart and enjoy the poems of **Jim Standish**. A veteran of the Beat Generation of poets in New York and a vibrant figure in California poetry circles today, Jim stands as an outrageously sane and compassionate man in an increasingly insane and intolerant world. Not without strong messages, he still infuses his poems with an infectious exuberance.

Another remarkable California poet with Northeastern roots is **Judith Bishop**, who has received numerous awards, including the *Five Fingers Review* 1991 Chapbook Award for her work *The Longest Light.* In recent years many of Bishop's poems reflect Native American concepts, which she has embraced for "a philosophy towards the earth that might preserve us." Her works included in this collection reflect her strong classical background as well as her personal and humanitarian concerns. For all the great pain manifest in her poems, Judith Bishop makes one realize the divine and hope-inspiring power of love, particularly women's love for their children, and a special sensitivity toward all that lives and grows.

Beautiful, rugged, indomitable Wales is worthily represented in this collection by **Richard Ball**, who, both as poet and poetry critic, is known and published throughout the English–speaking world. The great lyrical power of the villanelle "Hoofbeats"—just one of Ball's many fine works on the relentlessness of time—is reinforced by the galloping cadence.

Kevin Arnold, featured in the previous Zapizdat anthology, has also graced this one with his poems. Although his "Elmer Gantry Poem" offers a prime example of Arnold's quick and incisive humor, most of his works included here are more personal and serious. Readers with any experience of obsession should appreciate the raw power of "Driven," and the splendid cameo "My Parents Before Me" offers, in my opinion, the welcome example disproving an old cliché, for in all its nuances this short poem expresses more than a thousand pictures.

The poetry of **April Eiler** brings both delight and contemplation. Although a gentle, whimsical spirit pervades it, her work is not without profundity. "Dog-a-Roll" becomes a marvelous etymological tour-de-force built upon the many canine clichés in our language. "My Daughter the Seal" captures the serendipity both of children's animal fantasies and of the affectionate amusement and indulgence with which fond parents respond.

Lara Gularte also offers poems focused on the phenomena of consciousness over the human lifespan. She uses imagery, particularly food imagery, very effectively. As Eiler shows the bright side of parenthood, Gularte in her poem "A Mother's Nightmare" shows the "lion's tooth" that is also a reality of parental love—the ever-present fear that someone or something could abduct, corrupt, or otherwise alienate one's child; Gularte also implies powerfully that, no matter what, love prevails.

·**Beecher Smith** and **Peter Berardo** both offer pithy and well-crafted pieces. Berardo, in a litany reminiscent of the Lord's Prayer, recalls and presents the character of his own father, painfully and honestly, but not without appreciation. Beecher Smith celebrates the human condition in poems quite diverse in form and tone. Approximating the villanelle form,"Revelation" resounds with the eternal hope present with awareness of divine love; by contrast, "Debbie's White Christmas" resonates with despair in the depiction of a couple's life wrecked by a spouse's substance abuse which respects neither hopes nor holidays.

11

Another new contributor, **Scott Lowe**, also dares to employ lyric forms as well as free verse with skill and economy. Lowe gives one hope not only that the pen is mightier than the sword but also that the poem may be mightier than the petition for exposing abuses by the "Bully-Boys of the Banker Trade." Lowe has an appealing gift for irony and word-play manifest even in the titles of his poems.

Two taut, gripping poems by **Auriel Yost** relate with dignity and without overstatement incidences of insensitivity and hypocrisy which gratuitously compounded the suffering of one faced with life-threatening illness and hardly less arduous medical treatment.

Challenging and highly philosophical, the poems of **Wojciech Zalewski** expand one's consciousness through skillful antitheses and mythic allusions. The pervading atmosphere is that of great tenderness offset by a kind of fin du siècle languor. The references to pigeons in "Creating" seem to be alluding to the non–canonical legend of the boy Jesus' having amused himself by fashioning clay pigeons, then turning them into live birds.

David Harr offers some greatly overdue criticism of dogmatic and formulaic but uninspired approaches to "teaching" poetry. He too is one of a growing number of poets employing and enjoying lyric devices. Like Scott Lowe's "Bioillogical Blues," Harr's "Telegram to Nowhere" illustrates the psychological power of words for their author even when they may no longer have any practical effect on a damaged or difficult personal relationship.

Like snapshots from life or tapestries of history are the thoughtful, detailed, sometimes whimsical poems of **Dora Kushner**. Thoroughly American, yet deeply appreciative of her European roots, she offers the insights of her life rich in experience. "Springtime in Bruges—1520" exemplifies her fine sense of detail without either denigration or idealization.

A new and welcome voice in poetry, **Esther Kamkar** offers well paced, succinct scenes from her childhood in Iran and portraits of her loving relatives vividly recalled in her long poem "Connections."

Talented lyricist and linguist **Anatole Lubovich** offers an unusual treat: a verse translation of a poem by one of Russia's favorite twentieth-century poets, Sergei Yesenin.

Appropriately for a book published in December, this anthology concludes with three Christmas poems, one by **Carol Hankermeyer**, one by me, and one by Tomás San Andreas. I do not entertain the illusion that these poems will deliver anyone from cynicism or apostasy, but they will affirm that some of us still do believe in Christmas with a capital C and God (singular) with a capital G.

It seems inappropriate to critique my own poems selected for this anthology. Still, two observations are in order here: (1) Although the term "tema con variazioni" ("theme with variations") previously existed, heretofore it meant a poem constructed of quatrains, each beginning with the respective line from the first stanza, or even from the first stanza of another poem, especially a well-known one. My "Tema con Variazioni" is infinitely more complex because every stanza employs the same words found in the first stanza, only rearranged differently in each succeeding stanza. (2) The incident with Mario Lanza relayed in "Two Men in White" is based on newspaper accounts; the second poet is a composite figure embodying the ills of many but not intended as a portrait or caricature of any actual individual living or dead.

Finally, let me offer profound thanks to all the poets who contributed to this collection. Although the common denominator both of its contributors and of its readers is the English language, every effort was made to represent the greatest possible variety of peoples and cultures. Those not represented were omitted, not through exclusion, but simply by default.

Vassar W. Smith
December 1, 1993

MARTIN HOLROYD

Martin Holroyd

Spring Song

Now rise green enchanters
Sign of feather-dressed ranters
Mark deep the melting snow

Milk-white mistletoe
Cut from oaken groves
Has wound through the rite
And time
Turning to the light
Will unfreeze flowery wives
Of the weave around their thighs

Warm winds of the south
Will blow out
Cold words from her mouth

Now bow the lovers
After the long cold cull
With offerings to the ovary wood
And the rushing streams
Of the fertile blood
The rising rustling symphony
In hail and praise
Of the one green deity
And the fall of winter

GENERATIONS

Paint Box Poem

Key up the pitch
Make syntax rich
High palette noble sound
Slap on Van Gogh
Truest of blues
Splash primaries
All around

Strip yellow out
From Cézanne's sun
Rip black
From cloistered night
Chlorophyl green
Squeezed summer scene
Before pristine
Antarctic white

Fire Gauguin red
Straight to the head
Force Polynesian sky
Cerise Matisse
Pinkest of inks
Splash primrose
On soiled dye

Paint cobalt in
From Seurat's sea
Taint poems
In brightest hue
Braque's bouncing brown
Clowning around
Makes the palest
Prussian dark blue

Martin Holroyd

On Words in Poetry

Where's the loud chroma of my words
They hang like thin cold madrigals
Among the dusty colours of glory
Limp from the long original shout

Born from the pit of night in the throat
Each crippled character is bent
Stripped of flesh on the journey out
Its bones achromatic in the light
Borrowed and abused and re-learnt by rote
Twisted, diminished, a thousand drones

I cannot glory on original construction
When the coats of tarnished colour peel
Words are revealed in their underwear

Well-heeled selection again in gold leaf
Their innocence sold to me every time
A tempting vanity would make me a thief
To think they could be a perfection of mine

GENERATIONS

The Devil's Mistress

The snick of the latch
Announces his presence
(She loathes him in daylight)
Detesting herself
For loving his darkness
The depravity they share
Silently
He steals in
To stretch fantasies
Beyond her boundaries
And quench desire
In her thatch of nerves

Romance for My Children

Now the artless phosphorescent sea
Fired up the romance in your eyes
In a shell tucked to your ear
You heard the legends in the tides

Not now the bone-white artifact
Knocked on flint and iron
The mirrors of your dreaming eyes
Show Caldey as old Avalon

For where you stand upon the bluff
The oldest song sings in the bay
You saw the sail on Arthur's barge
Cross water where Excalibur lay

And in Camarthen by Merlin's hill
Or on Pembroke's windy ridge
Pendragon's pennants over Dyfed flew
And his fame to far Carthage

So when you go, my children
Into the electronic rigmarole
Make a small room for romance
In the land they call your soul

And think on this when weary
In the machinery's neutral shift
There was a time when romance
Was this child's greatest gift

GENERATIONS

A Poem of Many Colors

A poem of promise sweet as a plum
A gripper that grips like a fig
And a poem to make the heartstrings hum
And one dry as a judge's wig

A homily as heady as ancient wine
A rollicker that rolls off the tongue
And a poem to make a sweetheart mine
And one from which agony is wrung

A jingle so juicy ripe like two pears
A thumper that thunders on and on
And a poem where technique recurs, recurs
And one so boring the reader has gone

If you are sated by the satirical skit
I'll roll in alliteration and rhyme
If you are unified by university wit
I'll soak in pears, plums, and wine

Swans

Two swans drum
To low gold sun
Flying upriver
Their wings unison
Together in time

Silent they sing
Vows on the wing
Faintly quiver
A united ring
In eternal climb.

GENERATIONS

Cold Stone Rose

An inmate in the asylum
Talks to the cold stone rose
Put there by a simple craftsman
Whose chisel stopped long ago
Latched to the perfect petal
The shape and solid form
Bring to amorphous fluid mind
An island near the norm

Some Men's Wrath

In ragged moonrake froth
The memory hauls
Vague scented forms
Of girls I knew
(Who knew more than me)
And gave generously
Seminars
In seminal drills

Rerunning skin-flick stills
Stirs some men's wrath
They could not school
Those whirlwind whores

Where tossed
High beached and hurt
Upon their own remorse
Trying to halter
A wild sea horse
And never learned
The rule of a girl
Dressed in a pagan skirt

GENERATIONS

Holy Spring

High in the air of a hill
Away from the rosey ring of children
When a rainbow stood still in the sun
And nature's silence came to my side
I hear the soothing sayings
The music of my holy spring
The gurgling and cooing
The pre-natal pool
The upwelling tide
Of the unconscious
That fill the cracked panes with love

My factories of desire fade under the flood
And the unknown blow of the soul's growth
Will shove the stopper of my design aside
And the clean fountain of the spring
Will unpollute the river of this man-made mind
And my unshackled soul
Pure as a bell will ring
In the washed winds of the heavens

Choirboys and Cowboys

Winter
Nineteen fifty–four / fifty–five
Scrubbed Sunday boys sledged
Slid and snowballed home
Angelic voices raucous and alive

White surplices hung surplus
Silent in the vestry
Cold, stiff, stern
And under Victorian glare

Where are these yesterday heroes
Who giddy-upped Cassidy
And Hoppalonged home
To roast beef range
Buttered scone and Lone Ranger
Firing off their six-gun fingers
Up and down the street

Then out again to meet
There… by snow dens
Trees and dammed streams
Where no black-hatted stranger
Lingers and walks
Lassoing our dreams
And who never talks
Of Cisco and Zorro

Tomorrow, tomorrow
Let the sour stranger come
And catch our snowy hands
Lead us up the cloudy canyon
From our joys and toys

Now cold Sundays echo
With ghostly choirs
In a town of old cowboys

GENERATIONS

Night Games

At the dark node of night
The small, furred flurry, and cries
In the day-warmed grass
And quick shuffle by the hutch
The badgered house sighs
There is shifting in the joists
With the cooling crack of age

Is it silence at my table I hear
Or wine singing in the glass
And the crash of a turned page

Perhaps tinnitus
Ringing in my declining ear
Or St. Vitus dance of ivy leaves
Shingled in the moon
With the scuffle of moths at the sash

Smoke dreams up from my pipe
Drifting layers in the room
Smelling of briar and ash

Images and words tumble in my head
Innocent as fox cubs under the shed

Perhaps the fruit is ripe

I'll stumble over phrases and time
Tinker with noises, shadows, and scents
And make a rough but running rhyme

Forty Year Dash

The time light crossed my eyes
I was running
From egg and seed
Full tilt to manhood
Taking any prize
Being brash
Managed to stretch a lead
Most ambitions achieved
I thought to take stock
Relax awhile
Perhaps trust more to luck
Leave time for the energetic
To pace the clock

Looked back
Only to see death
Catching up

GENERATIONS

Stroke

"I can manage,"
He snapped
Explosion between us
Bloodclot bomb in the brain
Caused furious
Wintry numb feeling

Years later
Sat dumb
Wrapped against cold
I couldn't feel
He cried
Help with primary needs
Exhausted pride

His anguish over
I soon feel cracked
Hearing the same racked sobs
Echo again
Round the bathroom

Martin Holroyd

Private Ceremony / Cwmdonkin Park

A small cold wizened day
Drizzle blown gusty from the bay
Smooth wet stone with words
Time, green and dying
Amongst the trying tall blooms
And spring water blubbery

I don't know what I expected
There was no smell of woodbine
From the shrubbery
On tunes from the chimneys
Or, "Hey, Mister!" in the slant groves
Only two hunchbacked men
Playing bowls on a damp lawn
The knock of their dull woods
Detonating now and again

Feeling slightly foolish
I'd climb this lank hill
Assuming something Olympian
Only to find a stone
A folly among wet sad flowers
Small sterile chiseled words

O but on reading
The sounds they made
Like a sermon from the mount
Singing as tall bell towers
In the wind

Alone for one small moment
I touched the stone
Softly, as a blessing or wreath
Turned to face the sea
And walked the twisting turning paths
To Swansea Town beneath

GENERATIONS

Christmas

Under the last mad Christmas star
In muffled love across gooseflesh snow
Drifting to the yule log house
Round the caroled lanthorns glow

Under the mad gad mistletoe
Bustled girls give a berry-red kiss
Round the table men carouse
His spirit in Christ's genesis

Under the last glad tiding bliss
Anchored Son sees future derision
The family dog yawns in his paws
As Christmas goes past on television

Martin Holroyd

The Returners

A chill comes down from the door lintel.

We pass through.

Little we can say or do
can make a warm welcome from the stone floor.
Dry rot has run rippling through the woodwork.
Rain makes damp circular stains on the ceiling.
The mantle is broken (maybe vandalized)
and the paint is peeling
where lace, needles, brass knickknacks
other odds and ends of a life
gleamed gold in the lamplight.
Or plates leaned warming on the fireplace
when our life was simple and good.

Clinker in the grate is old.
Grime crusts the tiny window.
Time tracks a betrayal of trust.
A gray voice of dust tells us to go.

But, grave promise and wish leave no choice.
Memories flash out of the past to magnify our woe.
No other uncontrolled act for grief we know.
There's no gate nor stile for a return.

It's time, my brother,
to sprinkle the ashes from the urn.

GENERATIONS

Poem for Emma Jane

If I could dispel the pall of winter
Unbutton my suit down to birthday one
Double back autumn's fermenting apple
Unberry the bush in the vat-eyed sun.

Again push spring in the velvet tunnel
Let summer illuminate pelvic night
May two blue eyes and new longing senses
Awake for the songbird in morning light.

Exploring finger feel out tiny textures
Watching a spider silk a farmyard wall
Breath milky air in the dewdrop morning
A school lane lover among hedgerows tall.

I would run again those purple heathers
Sherbet and rockpool by a coastal town
Find woodland acorn on churchbell Sunday
And good-night story as the sun goes down.

Revel in corn in a warless country
I'd glory in faith and the fairy tales
Harvest holiday or star-born Christmas
By a timeless mother before time fails.

Dear Emma Jane would you rebear the pain
The fire, the pummeling of my rebirth
For I would live again loud days of spring
In your sweet loving and gift of the earth.

R. CLEMENT WOOD

Death of the Fourth-Grade Teacher

After the mazy ordeal, seminars, papers,
critiques of the fellows stinging with rivalries,
divorce from Nancy (herself bent to a doctorate),
Andrew will emerge from his humbling concealment
In a strict square hat with a tassel of gold.
Admiring the stripes of his gown, he is modest,
he is grateful, he is urged to assurance
that will last till retirement when he gets a job
and writes the books. The books! Drawn from the well
of his begetting, his books (he is sure) will be solid
as bed-earth where his poor farmer forebears lie
expecting Great Things from their Andrew.

But the day of Commencement where his gown
droops with sweat and his thoughts turn to Nancy,
his mother casually tells him that Miss Ada Brown,
an old grade-school teacher, has met with an accident:
she was crushed by her own car at the gate
to the farm where she lived with her invalid father.
The handbrake had failed, and the car lumbered upon her.
She had taught the fourth grade at Mount Carmel School
for thirty-five years. Eighteen of those back
Andrew had been a pupil of hers. Now she is for him
a tall smoke, a gaunt frame in the shiny
blue dress that Andrew'd supposed she never took off.
She was a function, a vague form at the blackboard,
a voice of the paradigms, a finger on maps.
Other teachers sought love and they got it,
an affair of some months. Miss Brown never asked,
never got (it seemed) so much as that.
It is a wonder that now he recalls her at all.

Tonight he is aching for Nancy. He has a strange
dream: a magician in tails with the face
of a sneering grad-school professor has Andrew
on stage in a chair. He blows smoke in his face
and invites the audience to laugh. He waves
a wand at Andrew's forehead, and lo, there runs

GENERATIONS

out a blue dress which lies in a heap on the floor.
The magician blows smoke, and suddenly Miss Brown
fills the dress, she rises, she bows. She walks
off the stage without looking at Andrew, whose eyes
now are crossed. He is drooling and blubbering.
The magician cries,"See how the loss of his fourth
grade has made him an imbecile. All his diplomas
all his degrees are from this time rescinded!"

Andrew wakes up, knows he is still a doctor,
but he will lie sleepless for hours in grief
for Miss Brown. Her worn-out old car rolls over her body,
rolls over again until nothing remains
but a patch of blue cloth to reflect the dawn's light.

Mack, Ernest, Willie
Early '30's, Mississippi Delta Country

1.

Until I was six
I lived in a city,
came to the cottonfarm
in shorts and a beret.

Suddenly I plunged
in a world of ancestors,
I put on the overalls,
took on the chores,
learned not to speak
except when addressed.

O sadness,
that was a beginning
of sorrow and joy
for the son
of a father
down on his luck,
having to live
as a poor-relative tenant
at the beck
and the call
of an uncle-by-marriage
on a wide cottonfarm.

O that wide cottonfarm
of those days:

the farm held in hock,
the uncle in whiskey.
God in Your Mercy
give drink to that soul
in Your cottonfield
where it labors
and sweats.

GENERATIONS

2.

Sing *Eleven-cent cotton, forty-cent meat,*
I carried the water down to the fields
where the people were picking, a hundred
men and women, and some of the children.
They did not sing like fieldhands in movies;
they talked low to themselves sometimes, sometimes
would laugh, picking so well and so fast
I could not follow close with my little
make-shift flour sack. At the most I could pick
about fifty a day, my fingers all bloody,
knees aching from clods. *Their* fingers
were tougher but knees, backs hurt them worse:
at the end of a day some could not
straighten, walk a straight line. Not one
of them ever looked at me, spoke any word
to me. I'd put down the water-jars. From those
they would drink, the water gone hot by that time.
There were heroes among them, sometimes a woman
weighing in for the day with five hundred pounds —
always somewhere near that — and where they
had worked, row after row, the bolls
were picked clean. *Now* try to do the job clean,
you god-damned clumsy cotton-picking machine!
Sing *Eleven-cent cotton, forty-cent meat.*

3.

Among all the people who worked on that farm
there were three whom I thought that I knew,
handy-men, dandy-men, they lived on the place.

There was Mack, a dignified elder and driver,
and Willie the swarthy with scar beading his throat,
and there was Ernest, young, tall, with big hands,

and I with them riding a mountain of cotton
adrift on a cloud above the hot asphalt
as the mules felt the strap and pulled for the gin.

Of the three only Ernest patted my shoulder
and gave me to know I was all right with him.
The strength rippled his body, he had a good wife.

Stiff as a ramrod, Mack held the reins
beneath a tall hat, round, with no crease.
They said he was Indian, like a chieftain he looked;

this was his land, he in loneliness owned it.
Nothing so low as mere scorn rode in his face,
stony, impassive his mastery. I humbly gazed.

Willie would glower at me. I'd catch him at that
and then he would change and flash me a grin
made of three tushes that could eat me alive.

Those men had their being which reason can't know.
Mack, Ernest have grown upward, commanding the sky,
but Willie's my Haunter, I'm afraid of his face.

Note: A popular song heard on records wheezing and
wobbly on the wind-up Victrolas some of the better-off farm
families had in the '30's was *"Eleven-cent cotton, forty-cent
meat,"* a whine of the Depression conditions.—R.C.W.

The Cruise

Barney's mother scrimps for years
to have him go with her
on a caribbean cruise, a travel-
package deal. Aboard you eat
a ton of food and go ashore
to shop. The *Norwegian Star*
is but to him a plastic yo-
yo winging on a finite string
out here, quick there, and there
a straight skid home. And so it is
predictable, a regulated
safe-house with casino
out to sea. "Have fun," the cruise-
director wheedles. "Come to parties,
get a case of rum, a fine Swiss
watch, a world-class camera duty-
free." Barney's body is confined
to ship and tour, but he yearns
outward to an eidolon of beach,
a stretch of alienated Cuba maybe,
then Hispaniolan peaks, red
dawn at harboring, ramshackle
moorings at Cap Haitien. Black
ragged sails like Moorish flags
close in behind, and naked boys
swim alongside the *Norwegian Star*
crying in their patois for his change:
Içí, papa hey you papa-man!
A duanier stands stiffly
in his white uniform. Extras
loll about the customs-sheds
in bright bandanas. Far to left
the tall brute butte of Jean
Christophe, too terrible
for France. To right, close by
a stuccoed church. Farther right,
an estate-house with its pool and walls.
Dazed, he and his mother walk
the quay into the marketplace,

plucked and torn at by a vending
horde. They emerge arm-laden
with odd souvenirs: an embroidered
shirt, a skinny wooden godling
whose gaze a white man dare
not follow *à le lent chemin de Guinee.*
Barney's body, back on board, will swim
will have rum punch, will pluck
the mountain of the midnight feast.
They will be moving on the lucid sea;
they will be slotted safely home.
His wife will startle at the wooden
statuette. "My God," she'll say,
"Wherever did you get that?"
They will laugh and put it
in the attic. He'll be drawn
to pay it many visits through the years.

GENERATIONS

Business Recession — Early '70's

Mr. Hankins swivels all day in his barber-chair,
Watching TV and waiting for custom with hair
On its head. So much of his custom is dead,
His two younger barbers left who had said,
"The wearing of beards and long hair is a fad;
We'll hang together while business is bad,"
But they finally left him alone in his shop
Until I came in asking an inch off the top,
Light trim at the sides. He says he knows
The wrongs of the world as his clipper mows
My head to the quick, forties-style, nearly bald,
And runs water so hot on his towel it'll scald
My flayed neck. He says the country's gone to hell,
Drugs and all that, guvment can't tell
Him what to do, regulate him, make him a goat.
He stares out the window with his blade at my throat;
I make no argument with the press of his steel,
I am still, stare at him, at the street, at the reel
After reel of long-haired men and boys shuffling by.
He lotions my skin, whisks me off with a spry
Motion. I leap to my feet. I see in the glass
My peeled head, a little boy's face. I quickly pass
A hand to my wallet, but Hankins' not there!
My heart starts to knocking, I look everywhere,
But he's gone. I am alone in the darkening shop:
Cars. people, barberpole spin like a top.
O the loneliness! Hankins slips out the back door,
And I ponder an old pile of *True* and my hair on the floor.
Murdered witches, mad badgers rage in the skies
That sent Hankins packing. Hoping to exorcise
The insanity, I cross myself and wait in his shop
Till I am covered with hair and time has to stop.

Bethel to Peniel

> *"The stairs were such as whereon Jacob saw*
> *Angels ascending and descending, bands*
> *Of Guardians bright, when he from Esau fled*
> *To Padan-Aram in the field of Luz,*
> *Dreaming by night under the open Sky,*
> *And waking cri'd, This is the Gate of Heav'n. "*
> — *J. Milton, Paradise Lost, III*

"Another Christmas, oh!" this old fellow groans,
So many strivings, rivalries, heart beating time
Time time to say the end is coming but not yet."

On the last Sunday of Advent he has dragged himself
To church and heard them sing "O Come, O Come,
Emmanuel" and a flinty Bishop preach the fall,
Man's old sick selfishness, and Man"s wrenching need
For his Redeemer. He remembers how he cheated Esau
Of his birthright, how he fled how one night,
Head on a stone, he dreamed of stairs with angels
Wafting up and down, and at the top Great Light.
(The place was Luz. all right, and worthy to be called
The House of God, he thought.) The rest was trouble,
The long delay until he should come home to face
Expected retribution. Guilt and fear, the deadly lot!

Brooding before bed, tumbling in the bed, he dreams
A gigantic man of muscle had half-throttled him.
Tossed him to the floor, pinned him, counting in a voice
Of thunder. With one hard kick, he rolls from under him,
But not before a huge hand dislocates his thigh.
Awakening, he knows his arthritis has got worse.

Still, everything has changed this year for Advent,
For his coming Home. His brother strides to welcome him,
And after dinner he goes in to see his newborn
Grandchild, plump despite the hardships of the road.
Later he will hold this child and hear his daughter
Say, or some voice emanating from her say like song:

GENERATIONS

"Father, you are mental, intense, a worrier;
Ease yourself, and join the generations wafting up
And down. Love, I've heard it said,
                    is a durable fire
            In the mind ever burning:
            never sick never old never dead
                        from itself never turning.'"*

---

* From the final stanza of Sir Walter Raleigh's *"As You Came from the Holy Land"*

J. C. WATSON

Kate

Jolly's what you seem
with your laughter, too loud for a lady.
You're big, but there's no mistaking
the fineness of your face bones,
the high persimmon blush,
the poured cream forehead,
the still alive rusty brown curls.
Those sky blue eyes spark with wit,
but always keep some secret, even from yourself.

You grew up before I did,
sprouted peach tipped breasts and womans's hips,
and strode into the world.
But your eyes and mouth never spoke the same language
except when crossing from tipsy to drunk
you'd say,"oh my," voice trembling,
eyes glancing at your shoe tip,"oh my."

Outside your house terrible faces leer;
it is winter in the center of every night
when you wonder if there'll always be a man to want you,
come from a wife's bed or a midnight shift.
come and scratch at your window or love words into your
                                                    breast.
I can see you on the hole-chewed couch
reading, after the kids have gone to sleep.
the history of everything, and you make sense of it,
explain the whole insane story
of this world of fools and cannibals.

Don't laugh so much; don't let them eat you.

GENERATIONS

A Story You May Forget

There is nothing here—well, the city,
but nothing you might want to look at with more than a
                                         glance.
Nothing in these beginnings except
the sufferings you have read about in every novel
and, therefore, the crying from these stones may be ignored.

The twisting streets need not be construed as metaphor.
The woman, my mother, young and old in the freeze-frame
                                       doorway,
dead baby inside her, hanging on with prehensile
                                    strength,— this
could be any woman like her... like her... like her.

So, let us not make anything of this: there is a Milky Way
                                     of poor,—
no one face of which will ever gloss the cover of any
                                     magazine.
The jacket, the hat, the sleeping bag, the tackle box, of
                                     this man,
my father or any poor man, are mended with the silver tape
with which he wraps the cleaned carpets in the basement.

And such a parade of siblings, each with his own novel for
                                     his life.
Each heart-ripping day compounds their ordinary sorrow
so that there is nothing to tell through miraculous teeth
on the eleven o'clock news.

Nothing more dull than the vision of the myopic poor,
no circle more exact than their paths.
To anyone with anything to decide, the world's a puzzle,
but for the poor (and these poor) all doors open
into the very same room.

J. C. Watson

The Fisherman's Wife

Swims out of sleep
from her white lake of solitude
toward the flat heat of a morning
too warm for tea.
She licks at the cut lemons,
studies the roundness of the bread,
takes her knife and pares a slice
from the loaf's center,
winces from the bite of crust.

The hours pour slowly,
thick honey over her limbs
till from the peach evening
he comes with the catch,
flicks the scales with his curved blade.
They fall, transparent coins on the paper
bland with old news.

Melting butter in the heavy pan,
she hums,
placing notes in the enveloping silence,
the sizzle of cooking fish making chorus
in the purpling room.

At table
slices of fish slide,
go sliding down the fat wife's throat,
beneath the skin
pale and rippling as a hen's.

She washes their plates in the soft stream of water
while the fisherman sucks from a large
carved pipe, and thinks of his day:
the placing of bait on the hooks
just so,
the small slice into water,
the bounty, the stretch of arms,
the steaming, buttery flesh.
He watches the woman through smoke
as she turns down the quilt.

GENERATIONS

Husband,
Wife,
lie on their backs floating,
their hands soft with the oil of fish,
hair cloudy gray;
they catch each other's hands in the dark.

The fisherman's wife stares,
and staring, wonders
if she will be like the others,
her eyes round and open
when she is dead.

J. C. Watson

Fate

People say that fate is in the wind,
that a man may find himself a fisherman,
while inside him is the priest
who has been blown to sea,
and for that man
the sea is his new religion.

The Fates are humming and weaving.
They have hearts like clocks:
everything must be moved
according to agreement.
You can't argue with time.

And a girl
may dress in a stiff-circled slip
and know she is a dancer,
but the Fates cluck and tick
and blow her into the lost black folds of a nun.

The Fates' hearts are so regular
they cannot imagine passion
so that a philosopher
places nozzles of gas into cars
all his life,
his brown silk hair a wound of fumes.
Yet he began with old books in the attic
like any thinker.
But those three mouths... blow!
And he is blue-fingered, green-greased,
black-fingernailed man
with unremembered dreams.

I knew a fat man;
he was a clown.
He could jump into the air,
sticking one leg forward and one leg backward
at the knee
so that anybody sad would smile
and anybody not would laugh.

53

GENERATIONS

But what he did
was sell Hoovers
door after tedious door
till he died at the wheel
of his parked car
on a sunny afternoon.

We read about the man
who stands atop his hill
and says, "I am where I want to be.
I am what I want to be."
And we wonder:
Is satisfaction an illusion?
Or do some escape
from the witches' wind?
It's that one thought
that makes the night
alive.

J.C. Watson

Song for East Palo Alto — Before the Wall

For our serenity,
the highway is edged in nameless greenery.
In the empty places where the slum leaks through,
boys paw the dirt in front of a fortressed store.
Pregnant girls walk no where.
Old men — if we stopped, we would see their eyes.

Thankfully, we are verdantly shielded
from that people-zoo, the foraging,
the raised-haired pacing of youths.
With lightning speed, our sturdy non-old vehicles bolt,
our radios tuned to the wars of Central America,
exotic hungers.

It's hot over there:
people gather under parched trees
to sing what's left of their language.
No one rides a bike.

Big sign in big letters over the leaning building
pretending to be a church: "God is."
Busy. I answer. As am I.
Scared. I answer. As am I.

I lived on a highway where the buses roared by,
black grit on the window panes.
Used to hear the train in the distance
in the middle of the night,
made me hurt all over.
But I was the right color for change.

No more their water and ours.
No more their bathrooms and ours,
their lunch counters and ours,
back seats on the buses—
stand to let me sit down.

GENERATIONS

Just their town and ours
and this highway slicing through
with not enough bushes
to keep out the nowhereness,
the blind corners,
dead ends,
of every street and alley
of my brothers' lives.

J. C. Watson

The Man Who Loved Glasgow

Waiting for you in the gray, persistent, dank.
Gray, lean the buildings.
Gray, the shipyards just ahead.
Gray, drips the sky onto your shoulders
as you approach.

I have come to find you.
It's three o'clock;
everyone who wants to be somewhere is there
and it isn't time to be somewhere else.

You are a heavy man; you wear a heavy coat
that sucks water from the fog.
No gloves or hat—in that you haven't changed.
Your hands are in your pockets.

I know what they press, release, as you walk,
your eleven keys (is it still eleven?)
and your father's watch. Each time you take it out
you hold fast to the lie of father-love.
You check the time, then you check your wallet,
counting the sad bills.
You want to be sure.

Ah, now your hidden eyes see me,
smile as you smiled at the ship
with your name on its bow.
Once I wore "Henry O." on my chest;
once I slid into harbor, obedient and cold.
Now you are gray as this city.
Your arms close, certain around me;
your face is not.

GENERATIONS

I won't ask if you walk along the Clyde each night
to take a pint at Gerry's.
I don't want to know.
If I do, I'll understand less
why we couldn't buy a car or have a holiday.
Or why you never spoke in the morning.
Why, when we'd go out walking,
your hand would come out of your pocket,
stroke the buildings as we walked along.

J. C. Watson

Girl Brushing

She sat brushing her hair,
for she was a girl after all.
Arcing forward, the red and brown
spread in fuzzy sheen
as the last sunblaze
impressed itself
upon the ivory walls.

She was a girl;
she could bend
in a blue satin robe,
her ivory neck
still a secret unkissed,
the brush crackling,
the snowflake lace
at the window
filling, going slack,
filling, going slack.

On her pillow wait forgotten dolls.
From the shelves the horses and stars fall down.
Young men, still round from childhood,
newly flower the walls.

When she leans down to brush,
she repeats the form of sorrow.
The satin robe folds.
Her hand works, small,
working through the heavy electric cloud.

For she is a girl
these mere seconds,
toes already
into a harsher land.

GENERATIONS

But for this moment,
a rare mercy:
only a girl brushing,
painting herself
into memory
against the saffron wall.

Time stops;
we who love her
hold our breath.

CHARLOTTE MUSE

Poets

We must learn to seem empty
like the sand the world leaves its tracks on,
or the field where the battle was.
A short time afterwards, the sea has swept in,
the earth has licked blood from itself
and groomed the long grass risen from flattened places.
Already a bird sings,"didn't-see, didn't-see";
and a deer grazes, lured there by the promise of emptiness.
"You are the first," the field says, knowing
that beauty depends on an illusion of stillness.

Clouds on the surface of a great firemarked clay bowl
kept to hold water.
When the bowl is empty, it holds shadows.
In a house framed by leaves where lizards run the walls,
someone sings the right song for the evening.
Now the young men who play the bear
at the caged windows of girls feel less foolish,
the policeman at the corner near the cantina grows
                                                    expansive.
Into the darkening sky goes the ball the children toss,
round like the night in the eye of a fish diving upward.

Let's live at the same speed as the things we watch!
We'll sit on the screened porch in steady moonlight.,
feeling the chair beneath us, the things that stay.
We'll tell our stories,
aware that without the house and ourselves
there is only the dangerous, mosquito-ridden night.
We won't become empty, no matter how many times
we say 'death,' or how many times
we smooth our faces to attract more life
and — not moving, not moving —
wait to see what replies.

GENERATIONS

In Alaska

On a rough beach
wrapped in stillness
a finger of rock is pointing at
a ragged piece of driftwood lying by a larger rock.
Then more stony sand,
a wild river.

I'd come there to see white mountain.
and icebergs roaring and turning blue insides out to the light.
I would have preferred to ignore the rock finger,
but what we see makes us responsible for it.
I watched it change, before my eyes, into a ridge,
then become a finger again,
then a ridge

The rock told me that it could be pointing, or it could be
a mountain range. It knows the earth inside and out. It said
odd juxtapositions are in the world. It said the driftwood is
death.
It said, this is your mind.

If the water hasn't risen,
or a bear hasn't kicked it aside on its way to the salmon,
if a wolf hasn't dragged its dog's tail and uprooted it,
the rock is still there, changing and changing

Turning to Stone

Bones go last.

After the death bacteria,
hovering close and waiting,
find a way in,
each of the body's cells dies separately.

Liquids lose their boundaries;
they drain away.
The smell of rot fades,
the fleshy solids vanish into flattening mounds
furred with grass and melting leaves.

But bones lie hard and buried
for centuries
(not dependent, as flesh is, on water for their shape)
and then, at last, begin their crumble.

A few bones don't dissolve.
They turn to stone.

Only one or two
of all the bones in a likely place
make the transformation:
The reasons are mysterious,
but I believe their power to remake themselves
resembles
feeling.

What I've seen of hardening is
refusal.
I think somehow
those bones refuse to settle.

GENERATIONS

Every crevice,
every pore and knob
hardens in its place

And then, from wherever
bone-memory is stored
comes change

The Sun Muffled, the Pond Crowded

In the dull early winter light,
there must be a thousand birds. Gulls float and shed;
loose feathers drift everywhere.
Coots bob, passive, apparently not even hungry.
Glamorous and temporary Canada geese,
a flock of terns coming in on boomerang wings,
ducks taking off in muscular flight, wild pigeons —
all there, filling up air and water.

Ahead on the path, a man in black with a wide–brimmed hat
appears, walking away into reddish light.
The oily pond surface throws back no reflection,
black shapes fly in low,
the queer light and the crowds of birds don't
change though the man
comes on.

There's a strange suspense,
an increasing alarm of birds, the sun
sullen in spreading cold —
the world unable to bring itself to radiant power.

We think it might react. We wonder if the marshes
that gave up their sweetness to machines
will conspire with the rest of what's destroyed
to strike back. Surely they'll do more
than die.

Along the inlet, an abandoned building with
an old globe of the world visible through a dirty window
sinks into mud left by receding tide.
Though the sun warms through and the sky clears,
innocent and predictable as ever,
we're thinking, half in hope, of earthquakes and drought,
of the man in black.

GENERATIONS

A Poet at the End of the World

Here in the present, where I live, everything
holds still for my naming. I animate whatever I choose.
Do you see the power in this?
Nothing rushes past or pushes forward.
My passions are for
the lush body, the green scene.
No abstractions; nothing to die for.

But this time, I want to talk straight to some future
poet and say we know what we're ignoring.
It's not that we don't see it coming.
Something has stolen our fire.
I do something and then have delicate feelings about it.
Is this our failure? Did we take our eyes away?
We ask you to understand — it's not that we lack courage.
Connections have broken and each is alone. This is why
we only seem to see ourselves.

You have to watch out.
We've been driven here into this slower *now* —
so many of us saying *I* as loudly as possible.
We're trying to say we matter.
The man on the street—the man lying on the street—
can't say it. We refuse to go so quietly.

We're like the pilgrims who came for a miracle
at Fatima — all standing in the rain under their umbrellas
looking towards the place of a vision.
Some say the sun turned in the sky, or at least shone
                                        strangely,
and that everyone who was there saw something.

JIM STANDISH

At the Races

A boy at the racetrack sees a man
drop his wallet. The boy picks it up,
looks inside: two thousand.
He chases the man, gives it to him.
The man grunts and goes his way.
All the boy's friends tell him he was crazy
not to keep the money. You must know
this is in America, in the time
of Reagan. In such places and times
people actually think like that, they think
the crazy ones are the ones who won't
sell their honor for two grand.

It should have gone like this: the man says
Hey thanks, here, you keep the money, I was just going
to spend it on horses anyway. But the boy says No,
I only did what folks are supposed to do, what should be
taken for granted. And the man likes this boy
so much, is so happy to find another soul
in this wasteland, that he says Tell you what,
let's arm-wrestle for it, loser
has to keep it. This tickles the boy, who plays
football in highschool and is sure he can beat
an old man, so he says Great.

But the man's strong, too. Soon
the muscles are bulging, the teeth are gritting, the arms
are not moving. Unnhh, unnhh, they both say.
Rrrr, rrrr, they say, and their sweat
is flying all over the place and still
the arms do not move. But at last, as it must
when strengths are equal,
the stamina of youth wins out. Okay,
says the man. Be a gracious winner and allow me
to take you and your family to dinner.

GENERATIONS

All riight, says the boy. All riight,
say his parents. The boy calls his girlfriend,
the father calls his newly divorced sister,
and they go to the fanciest restaurant they know of,
they order the fanciest food and the fanciest wine,
nobody cards the young people, they all get
very jolly, they go
to the hottest dance spot in town,
the boy and girl decide they're really in love,
the mother and father fall back in love,
the man and the father's sister fall in love,
they go to a swell hotel and take
the three swankiest suites.

Next day, the wallet's empty.
Best two grand I ever spent
says the man. Me too, says the boy.

Jim Standish

My Footnote

Ed Sanders, poet,
peace activist, Fugs singer,
was also editor & publisher of a mimeo mag called
Fuck You! / A Magazine of the Arts.

We met in Physics Lab. You couldn't miss him
as he plied the halls of NYU
with his Calculus book,
Greek dictionary &
Pound Cantos.

One night
we went to a party
uptown. The people there
were strictly bourgeois, so we made our own party
in the hallway,
giggling & rifling coatpockets for bottles
& taking one swig apiece out of each.
Oh, and there was
Scotch & Irish,
Canadian & Bourbon,
Brandy & Rum,
Gin & Vodka
to chase all the Chianti & Rheingold.

Erelong
I was filling that nice uptown bourgeois apartment
with wretched sounds of barf,
clutching the toilet like it was
a rock in the rapids
which it might've been the way the
room was reeling.
The hostess's best friend was going
"Aren't you ashamed,
a fine thing,
coming to a nice girl's party
& acting like a bum"
or whatever, you know
how it goes, & of course

GENERATIONS

I was ashamed,
I was mortified,
I kept going "I'm sorry,
yes I know
it's a terrible thing"
& she kept telling me to be ashamed
& I kept being ashamed
& she kept telling me
till I wasn't ashamed anymore,
I wasn't sorry anymore,
all I could think was
"Fuck You"
& I came staggering out of that bathroom sputtering
"Fu fu fu fu fu"

And right then
he tells me now, 30 years later, he had the name
for his magazine.
"You never told me that before"
I sez. "No," he sez,
"I never told you that before."

But now it's out:
my footnote
in the history of the literature of
the Beat Generation.

I wd also like to mention
how he seemed the world's only one that night
who didn't think me scum, & how
he took me gently in hand & led me—
all the way, saying "Calm yrself, calm yrself"—
down stairs & thru subways to my Chelsea room
& sed that's
what friends are for, which nobody
ever told me before.

Likely Story

Suppose you say
    there's a big fierce dog in the yard
        & a man goes in & there's
            a lot of snarling & the man runs out
                with his pants torn & his
                    leg bleeding

You haven't said
    the dog bit the man

Suppose you go on to say
    they treated the man for rabies
        & shot the dog

You still haven't exactly said
    the dog bit the man

Suppose you add
    for the rest of his life this man
        had a morbid fear of dogs

Even that isn't
    Dog Bit Man

For all I know
    a giant rat from hell
        materialized in the yard just as the man went in
          & that's what the dog was growling at
           & the rat was rabid & bit both
            dog and man

& this was all too much for the man
    so he blanked it out of his mind
        & fixated on the dog

So, if there's something you want me to know,
    best you come right out & say it.

GENERATIONS

Murphy's Law

I believe in God the
      Mother the Father the Child the
          Holy Ghost
             and Murphy
You know—the one
      who makes things go wrong...
But hey!—not always!

Every time a car doesn't
      jump the sidewalk & run you down
Every time you swallow a bite of something
      & don't choke
Every time the earth doesn't open up
      right under your house
Every time you speed & don't get caught
Every time you step out of the shower
      without slipping
Every time you forget your raincoat
      & it forgets to rain
Every time somebody likes something
      that you did
Every morning that you
      wake up—

Thank Murphy
      for his mercies. He says
we measly mortals have no notion
      all the things that could go wrong. He says
all blame & no praise
      make Murph a mean God.

Must Be Music

There must be music, cause
   mr sun & ms rain are doin
      a do-si-so, and the birches are swayin
         their long lissome selves almost like they could
            sashay right on outta town if they
               didn't dig it so much
                  right here!

Yes, there's music, it's playin
   all the time, wherever we go, even
      inside our very selves, never mind
         can we hear it or not
            over the shoutin & weepin,
               the marches & dirges, it's the
                  sweet hold-on shimmy of life,

so we'll keep on swayin with the birches,
   twirlin with mr sun, swoopin with ms rain,
      dancin away like our lives depend on it—
         cause probly they do.

JUDITH BISHOP

Lonely in America

The rim of the fountain
is cold under me,
my friends are late.
Still, I'm sitting in sunlight
and sea smell and gulls
breeze over
movies in the marsh,
concrete and the soul,
the white world, Malcolm X.

I watch black people coming,
about half the audience,
middle-aged, middle-class,
easy and confident,
wearing clothes like my own.
Teenagers, shy and noisy,
bang out of their parents' cars,
and the old walk carefully
towards history.

Lulamae Hopson,
I thought I was here for you.
After sixteen hours
of doing my mother's work
there was no one
to go back to your room for.
Alfred had died from his cigars
and your son was in Grand Rapids.
We often sat on your bed,
I would lean into your starched uniform
and we'd read together, talk about everything.
I was as lonely as you were
and felt you loved me
but wasn't sure as it was paid for.
At six I wasn't sure
if your color would rub off if I touched you
though your palms were as pink as mine.

GENERATIONS

Demeter Speaks
After the Pleiades Set in the Morning

I

As among your things
there was a new one,
I've put out the old salad bowl
half full of birdseed.

January in California
is cold enough,
the homeless desperate,
frost in the fields,
trying to sleep cold.

Being from the North
I didn't notice for years
but in this shabby house
I've come to
there is winter everywhere

and you have gone —
from your apartment, from the city,
the country,
from all contact with me.

II

We talked psychology for three hours.
You couldn't tell your thoughts from mine
nor tell me what you resented,
you want to own your own suffering,

and no king of hell
was taking you there now
though my father
had molested you
over and over.

A harassing tenant
where you lived drove you away
as November drives the leaves.
You took things deeply yours
and shed the rest.

III

I have gathered what you left
to me, and sorted the truckload.
For three days I talked with a dress
I'd given you that was never right.

I send Hitchcock chairs for repair
and fix your elegant desk and tables
myself, staining unveneered patches,
putting in new fastenings, oiling and polishing

the beat-up surfaces.
I fix the phone and the lamp,
restore the furniture
I, too, do not really own,

and take back my function
as matron, the one in the middle,
who does family business
and stores treasures.

Fifteen years ago I also took off
with my books and manuscripts
and left you to live
with portraits, silver, the family hoard.
Unpacking, I suddenly see the exchange.

I don't cry as I go among your things
left in drawers, the perfumes,
sweaters, photographs.
I keep sorting.

GENERATIONS

This is like a visit with you,
smells right, the textures
of old objects we've lived with
together. I haven't seen you in two years
though we've talked.
I look at a carved fan as I would your face,
touch scarves as I would your hands.

Your boxed papers I leave packed
and repack a small shrine,
an abalone shell, the Medicine bear,
spiritual images you may return to.

The grand piano fits
in our living room,
the chairs what we needed
for our dining table. How odd
to inherit from a daughter.

I use, for a while, lamp and phone,
a small tin of singer's lozenges,
some linen, then repack them.
All the rest, not outworn, broken, trash,
is stored next to your sewing form
with silk magnolias for a head.

IV

Restoring this order, what now
grows in me? More guilt
for my disposition of your things,
or less, for taking an older place
that frees you for new life?

What burgeons in me
is anger at being abandoned
when I have supported you
so profoundly,
the enormous costs
of your hurried desertion,

and utter grief
at loss of contact with you,
at my isolation,
fury that I must now make family
out of friends.

My original family
drove capacity for closeness
out of me. I have not stayed married.
Perhaps I am most furious at them.
Perhaps you are most furious at me
for not staying married and protecting you
from them, especially my father.
Married, I seldom saw them.

V

In Arcadia I was called the Fury
where the sea turned into horses
and ravaged me when I came
sorrowing for loss,
loss of my husband's love,
later, loss of my childhood
when my father had been good to me
and to remember that was disloyal to you.

It is hard to separate us two
though you are a singer and I write poems.
On the phone our voices are the same,
our handwriting, our energy,
our degrees of gift and discipline.
At times you have nurtured me, once I kept you alive.
She who generates fruitfulness, who is the fruit, the same:
Sheaf Bearer, She of the Seed, She of Green Fruits,
Heavy with Summer Fruits.

GENERATIONS

Persephone, she who brings destruction,
and Persephatta in Athens, she who fixes destruction.
I, the fruitful, am called the Sorrowful One,
planting called a kind of funeral in November
when the Pleiades sink in the morning at Eleusis.
I weep as the seeds go in the ground.

Those seeds of pomegranate:
what mysteries that call you back.
Last year you left also,
probably for Italy,
Proserpine, the fearful one.
I called for nine or ten days,
no answer. Were you dead?
Recovering can make one suicidal.

This year you have said
if you die it will not be by your hand
and I said don't get into situations
where it might be by another's.
Preserve your life.
And I believe, now, that you will,
though you go, periodically,
into your memory, into your suffering.

I live under a pine tree
whose quiet shade soothes
and my housemates comfort me.
Most of the day I write,
the rest of it make and tend gardens
that will grow our food and medicines,
learn, near sixty, how to care,
She of the Threshing Floor, She of the Great Loaf.

VI

You were snatched from my care
by hellishness,
as all the goddesses were raped
by the men taking over: Zeus, Hades, Poseidon.
Now, in war, an officer
says the fifty thousand women they rape
daily will win them the country.
The mourning of these women
does not save them.

Fruit Bearer, Wheat Lover,
I grow heavy
with all I must know.
My daughter is gone
and my awareness so increased
I no longer dance easily.

The poems, *pommes,* continue to come,
seasonless, the internal farming
digs deeper and deeper.
Is grief the light that transforms?
Whatever we feel must be known
or we rot. A man

works with me, as a gardener
prepares the ground. He
is more visionary, protector and support
than conqueror. We return
to thousands of years ago,
to the Mysteries, to hunt and gather
together our ravaged lives.

When you return to visit,
established in your self and life,
your mother and you
will laugh at those who confuse our voices
for we know how we differ
as all women do
who are not frightened of each other.

GENERATIONS

Holidays

Our relationship to the sun
four times a year
marks my holy days now,
however it is December twenty–fifth.
The morning light spears to my pillow.
Great Spirit, thank you for longer light and warmth,
the ceremony on Solstice,
closeness of friends, our prayers
and the feast and giveaway.

Last evening my beloved stepfather
who has been so ill and suffers so much
called me. I cried with happiness to hear him
and my mother, too, full of warmth.
After, my closest, oldest friend
had me over to dinner with her children
who had come to be with her.
We had oyster stew, sang carols,
trimmed a tree that died under the baubles.

Like the tree, I'm nearly done in.
On this night I do not know
where my child is. She has broken away
and I don't speak of it but my heart keeps stopping
like the clock at midnight when the animals speak.
These beliefs are so old in me I can't stop them,
responses as automatic as the Nicean Creed
I no longer trust or care about,
but on Christmas I am that god's child
as helplessly as being born.

RICHARD BALL

Hoofbeats

Hoofbeats still come trotting down the mind,
through crippled years that lost their metronome;
the tapping word and hoofbeat stand conjoined.

The reins of wisdom holding back behind
keep us in check, to stay still, but the lone
hoofbeats still come trotting down the mind.

To get out, and tell a story to the wind
is the poet's conscience, his horsy nature in the bone;
the tapping word and hoofbeat stand conjoined.

To saddle up, and be-damned, to beat the end
that dusts, and travels in the urn;
hoofbeats still come trotting down the mind

Here a tomb took the packaged poet, blind
stone the mason struck at,— "Horseman, pass on!";
the tapping word and hoofbeat stand conjoined.

But this swivel chair is the saddle now; here aligned
the reins of words steer the bridle of the pen;
yet hoofbeats still come trotting down the mind,
the tapping word and hoofbeat stand conjoined.

GENERATIONS

Group of Artists' Models, Circa 1791
(Painting by François André Vincent)

The blank canvas stands stiltified,
waiting, a lone sentry, looking out on
a vast space, A Doric column protrudes
out of the picture's base, on the ledged

window long dresses, billowing, gaudy
red ensigns, signifying art to be
accomplished, planned. A statue decorates
a plinth, surveying ladies in attitudes

interpreting their stares in oils.
Over the green baize stairway they drape
themselves on the decor, awaiting the
brush strokes to make an immortal picture

after death. The scene comes out of the
canvas, a parade, charged with history,
as though a gun-shotten discharge from
a culverin emptied itself into the air

and sprinkled fragments at the feet,
where guns blew bits out of the
galleons at Trafalgar, Nelson with his
wounds across the sodden deck. Where

historical fact is arranged like this,
the ancestral sweep of a brush is art made
for a specific purpose of depicting
centuries no longer in place, with

ourselves as lookers–on, wondering about
another century, which will pass away
like a conundrum, as time passes away when
we are lost, and emptied into oblivion.

KEVIN ARNOLD

Kevin Arnold

The One She Calls My Elmer Gantry Poem
— *For Brenda Hillman*

How we end up doing what we do seems random sometimes
With me, I knew a guy who owned this little TV station
And I talked him into letting me
Substitute a week for a weatherman on the 6 AM news

On Tuesday I forecast rain for Barstow
When it should have been Bakersfield
And was only a little surprised when that's what happened
Bakersfield had sunshine while
An unexpected cloud dumped an inch and a half on Barstow

No one noticed my power yet everyone
Thought I was a natural at being a weatherman
Whatever that means, so I got this weatherman job
In San Francisco and then New York, still mornings
—My personal life hasn't been too spiffy lately
I always wake up at four anyway—
So before long I started swapping spots
With Willard Scott on the *Today* show

My little power's never failed, but I use it sparingly
The only time I decided to do something big
Was with a hurricane but Willard had the first day
And the storm came in and hit Florida overnight
The next morning I put it back out to sea
So I helped the Carolinas
But it was too late for Florida
I guess I should have found a way to bump Willard that day

But you don't want to push things
I saw those floods coming and they were just too much
I figure I could have protected one city one day or something
But the entire Midwest, no, I didn't even try

95

GENERATIONS

A few have figured out
And tried to get me to help on the commodities exchange
You know America—but no
I use my power often enough, though,
If I know about a picnic or a wedding,
And a lot of the border states have
Their first snow December 24th—
You do what you can

They say I'm a good guy to know

Divorce Albums

At the bookstore on my planet
Next to the wedding books are divorce books
To capture forever lingerie from secret dates
A special occasion for the growing list of lies

A disintegration chapter for
The Christmas cards not sent
The children's lunches unprepared
The little blowups that infect the house

With a place for the counselers' and lawyers' bills
And the real estate commission statements
And photographs of the couple
In various stages of exhaustion, longing, even hate

An entire section for the day the kids are told
Pictures capturing their fractured faces
As their lives are changed dramatically
The two who brought them forth are irreconcilable

The planet provides leather binding and gold stamping
Of the books for those who reconcile
Wide publicity for the smiling faces
Of those who beat the odds

And the others always have their
Wedding and divorce books side by side
The wedding may have been for the parents but
The particulars of a divorce

The scarred children held in the middle of the night
The unexpected moments of cruelty and tenderness
The end of this they began together
This is theirs alone

GENERATIONS

My Father's Eyes
(For John B. Arnold, April 10, 1914—December 25, 1989)

Still I see my father's eyes
across formica from me,
long after I told him I would no longer deny
my mother's alcoholism.

They seemed to get glassier
in his seventy-fifth year,
when he asked me, from his heart,
why I couldn't forgive.

We both watched his hands shake;
still I held my ground,
mentioning four drinks a night,
mentioning pills.

He said, Son, it is the high point of her day;
don't deny her happy hour.
Suddenly, unexpected tears,
and his drawing his handkerchief

in that harsh California sunlight I had brought him to,
bringing the white cloth
slowly to his face,
lightly blowing his nose,

rubbing his eyes while I admitted
I was changing my part in our family game
pretty late in life—
he whispered: A Christian should forgive.

My mind jumped to the truths I wouldn't tell him:
I was jealous of his loyalty
(even if the self-help books had other names for it)
to this woman who had formed his life,

my mother, and because,
old, glassy-eyed, and shaking,
he had courage enough to confront me,
care enough to cry.

GENERATIONS

What Will I Be When You're Gone?

Bones I never see keep me erect.
Bones hold my brain in my body.
Bones never broken, not one.
Bones, what will I be when you're gone?

Bones are where blood is created:
Bone–marrows—mine weren't working right, so my Dad's
Bones took me to Sloan–Kettering, where they probed my
Bones with a needle-in-a-needle in my sternum. My
Bones sucked twice a week at first. My wrist and ankle
Bones were bound in leather straps, but my seven-year-old
Bones were so thin, I'd wriggle out. Then my
Bones were tapped while five or six interns held me down.
Bones of my father took me to Dodgers' games afterwards.
Bones of my father cremated four years ago—his
Bones were already burned when I learned. I was
                        shocked when
Bones were broken in a fight at Ebbet's Field—adults? My
Bones kept getting sucked until miraculously my
Bone–marrow made healthy blood again.
Bones, what will I be when you're gone?

Bones of the mummies with crossed arms. Their
Bones are what's left of them now. To preserve the main
Bone—the skull—they'd remove the brain through the nose.
Bones of my mother's skull, taken after a stroke. Her main
Bones couldn't hold her brain. The nurse whispered, Mom's
Bones are on floor three. Like my Dad's, my
Bones will be burned too—unless I object—
Bone–burning's politically correct.
Bones at the top of my head grow public now.
Bones is slang for a jazz pianist loose as jelly.
Bones and boners mean erections.
Bones, what will I do when you're gone?

Kevin Arnold

Driven

Perhaps one love is like another when it ends:
    only the one who wanted it to last
    understands what was at stake.

At least once you must have lived in that lovesick daze
    and glanced up to see someone who looked
    almost exactly like the lover who scorned you,

and didn't you jump up from your table, just to make sure,
    and run full–tilt wherever this phantom took you,
    driven by adrenalin, driven by hope?

And when. panting, you overtook this stranger,
    what did you do then? Were you apologetic,
    did you say,"Sorry, I mistook you…,"

or did you find the righteous power of the jilted lover
    and set things straight right then and there,
    describing the monstrous treatment you'd received,

you, who could have made it all work! Did you seize the
                              moment
    ·and tell the tale in that wonderful out–of–control
    desperate way that we only get to perform a few times

in real life, standing squarely at center stage for once,
    stating that, of all the people on this planet,
    you are one of the handful driven by love?

GENERATIONS

My Parents Before Me

This photograph of them courting in Charleston
The Dartmouth man sent south by GE before the war
A dark suit with a touch of white handkerchief
Her gloves held in her left hand, she looks
Unfettered, frozen in mid–step
Far from her mother on the farm
Downing pills by the handful
Her swaying, curvehuging beads give no hint
She will follow in her mother's footsteps
Her care will become his life
Just this snappy couple stepping out

APRIL EILER

Dog–a–Roll

A dog leads a dog's life
following its dog nose and dog ears
through dog days.
Its hair is the hair of the dog.
Its tail is the tail of the dog
and may also be an ingredient
that little boys are made of,
although dogs are never
made from little boys. They are
the form of patience
fashioned from wind and mud.
All dogs can talk, walk and work
like dogs.
In the end, they die like dogs
no matter how much we love them.
So let's give a cheer for the dogs:
top dogs, underdogs,
cool dogs, hot dogs,
sleeping dogs, singing dogs,
let lie, having their day dogs,
straw dogs, gingham dogs,
laughing-to see-such-sport dogs,
lost dogs. lazy dogs,
jumped over by the fox dogs,
mild dogs, mad dogs,
out in the midday sun dogs,
and wild, fey, sky dogs,
falling with cats in the rain dogs.

GENERATIONS

Dressing for Spain

It is all there:
sherry *oloroso,*
flamenco and the rumba *gitana,*
meandering in markets by day,
dark-skinned lovers at night.
You have only to dress.
Pull your jeans over your hips.
Arrange the tank top over your breasts.
Try.
Think of Laura del Sol
or the Duchess of Alba,
women bursting into bloom.
Don't change clothes again. Open the door.
Outside your walls you will find
ripe fruit offered with a smile.
Your hips will sway.
Your hands will open.
Your eyes will meet those of a stranger.
In time you will carry a basket on one shoulder
and swing gold charms from your ear lobes,
but now
all you have to do
is dress.

My Daughter, the Seal

Oh, the friendly flapping of flippers,
the playful high-pitched yelps!
Life with a seal
has never been easy,
but one makes sacrifices
for love.

Consider feeding time:
She rises on tail fins
and opens her mouth
while we toss sardines
that fall on the floor
and turn into popcorn.

Or, consider bedtime:
I hear the familiar slap-drag, slap-drag
as she pulls herself across the floor,
fresh from the bath tub, wanting only
to be hoisted to my lap,
caressed and sung
the Seal Lullaby.

> Sleep, sleep,
> Dream of the deep
> Straits of Alaska,
> Where no one will ask ya
> To brush your hair
> Or sit on a chair.

> Sleep, sleep,
> Soft, slippery mammal
> I'll love even if you
> Turn into a camel.

All things depend on tolerance
of creatures unlike ourselves.

GENERATIONS

Saraband with Mask

In the garden a masked man
bows to the rag weed
and brushes his cheek
on the petals of the iris.
It is dance and design
and hard work and so beautiful,
that the woman in the house
brings him fresh caviar.
He does not speak.
She feels ridiculous
and returns to her seat by the window.
Perhaps he will climb away over the wall
or disappear down a hole.
No one like to feel ridiculous,
but the man in the garden is constant.

So the woman talks
to the elves in her rafters
and eats all the food she hates.
She makes up rules like
no baths on Thursdays and
high-heeled shoes every Monday—
just in case it matters.

On the first day of winter
the masked man finally speaks.
He asks to stay in the house until spring.
Yes, says the woman, but first
you must show me your face.
The man takes off the mask and reveals
a face exactly like the mask.

In the spring he goes out
and bows to the rag weed.

LARA GULARTE

Madge

She was a brown-haired
middle girlchild,
soother, feeder of four brothers,
her mother's helper.
Feet laced tightly in work boots
stuck in adobe mud,
till the moss grew
between her legs
and she ran bare-legged,
barefooted, to the waiting
Fuller Brushman,
parked in his Packard
on a country road.

Two babies in two years
and the brushman away
door to door,
her feet grew swollen,
then flat.
When he left her,
she drank Port wine,
till something in the kitchen
grew fur and began to smell.
Peroxide
turned her hair orange,
and she got a factory job,
working nights.

At the change of life
she went on a grapefruit diet
and lost thirty pounds,
turned into a
beehive-haired blonde
in spiked heels, and
sold face cream,
drove a pink Cadillac.
Stricken with arthritis
at age 65,
she joined the church,
received healing,
and found Jesus.

GENERATIONS

Find her now
at the Senior Center,
bent and blue-haired,
in orthopedic shoes,
foghorn-voiced
high priestess of Bingo,
stalking dozing old men
with her cane,
cursing out soft-voiced
lady volunteers,
and telling anyone,
and everyone, about
the goodolddays.

Memory

Grandma Rose forgets names....
When I visited her last week,
She didn't know who I was.
Her todays slipping
just out of mind's reach,
she remembers herself best
in old-fashioned albums,
photographic memories
from yesterday.

My daughter couldn't remember
forgot that I took her
to Paradise Park once a week
when she was two and three.
She swears she saw the park
for the first time
on a second grade field trip,
wants to know why
I never took her there.

All day long
I stretch my brain
trying to remember my childhood.
Tonight I peel apples,
scrape away the soft spots,
core out the centers and
throw away the skins.
I pile white apple meat in a dish
and watch it all turn brown.

GENERATIONS

A Mother's Nightmare

In my sleep I chase monkeys...
Simian kidnappers have my child in a sack,
and I run fast to save him. Too late,
I watch helpless
as his arm is jabbed
with a syringe
and he grows fur.

I meet him now as a gorilla
and scream out the sound of his birth
when he squirmed wet and slippery
from my body to gasp his first air.
I ache again from the pain,
for he will no longer
be cradled in my arms.

Once he stood as high as my knee,
small hands reaching up.
Now we stand head to head, and
he turns away. When I awaken,
I will stand at the edge
of the great jungle
and wait for him.

BEECHER SMITH

Revelation

I know that a gentle age will come
    In spite of what the warlords say;
Those who endure will not stay dumb.

Though I do not know where from,
    Nor exactly on what day,
I know that a gentle age will come.

Brutality brings death to brutes, but some
    It killed, lived in a peaceful way;
Those who endure will not stay dumb.

Above the noise of the fife and drum,
    Beyond the notes of the march they play,
I know that a gentle age will come.

From the dread missiles and the atom bomb,
    Protect and spare us, dear God, I pray.
Those who endure will not stay dumb.

Though this world end at the hands of some
    Who will not trust in the peaceful way,
I know that a gentle age will come.
Those who endure will not stay dumb.

GENERATIONS

Little Hurts

It always comes time
for the little hurts:
the farewell at the door
without the goodnight kiss;
the expensive dinner tab
with nothing but a handshake
to show thanks for it.

Then come the larger hurts:
the you-don't-love-me
and I-don't-love-you-anymore hurts,
preceded and followed by empty lovemaking.

What happened after the handshake
which led to the goodnight kiss
which led to the affair
which let to the breakup?

Leave me with the little hurts
From which I can easily recover.

A Woman's Tears

She cried when I entered,
She cried when I went out.
She cried when she was certain.
She cried when she was in doubt.
She cried when I had money,
She cried when it ran out.
She cried when our love started,
She cried when our love was over,—
But she laughed when she departed
To take another lover.

Debbie's White Christmas

The gift of hurt
Keeps on giving:
Your last kindness
Consumed our Christmas Club account
Along with my whole week's wages.
At the hospital,
Where the expert medical staff
Repaired my face and your wrists,
They had nothing on hand
With which to mend hearts.

The emergency room specialist
Would not say that your alcohol
Was more powerful than his alcohol.
He had no drugs
To counteract yours;
No feelings
To fill the void of unfeeling
Caused from feeling too much,
Then forcing you
To dull the pain
With more substances.

As the intruding carolers
Inflicted "The First Noël" on families
Stranded in the waiting Room,
I brought the car around
To pick you up
And drive us back
Through the snowflakes,
Wondering
What home have we to return to
So long as you seek solace
In white powder and amber liquids?

PETER BERARDO

The Son's Prayer

My father, you are now in Heaven.
Honored is your name.
Your kingdom was your home
Where your will was done,
Keeping hearth for seven.
You gave me my daily bread,
But never forgave me my trespasses
As I forgive you who trespassed against me.
You led me into imitation
But kept me from evil.
For yours was the home
With the power and the glory,
Then. But not forever,
Amen.

Morning Sounds

Between cricket and bird songs,
Before the spread of dawn,
Under covers of darkness,
Amid sheets of warmth,
The best sound is:
"Good morning."

SCOTT LOWE

Scott Lowe

Banker Trade

They hauled me before the tribunal,
these bankers, plump of soul,
eyes flat and dead, these
bully-boys of the banker trade.

What are the charges? I asked
pink shirt blue tie. Have I assailed
the Federal Reserve or absconded
with funds from old-folks' homes?

No, I have asked for a loan at
seven and seven-eighths fixed,
and there on my record, neatly printed
(by calling up my social insecurity number)

Is my history in numbers, my history
in rows and columns, where I shopped,
what I bought, dates, places, color, make, and model,
my life as data at the call and beck

Of these bankers, bully-boys of the banker trade.
And what sin is splattered black on my record?
Late with six payments you say? Well, this is
serious: certain evidence of instability.

Perhaps even the outcrop of antisocial sentiments,
maybe a hint of something darker — worse than
violence — slowing down the profit machine,
and disrespect to these bankers, eyes flat and dead,
bully-boys of the banker trade.

GENERATIONS

Ozzie Something

A sure as the four food groups
build bodies twelve ways,
Harriet and I never made
smacking noises.

I'm absolutely certain I never saw
Harriet on her knees in the bathroom,
looking for her diaphragm.

And listen, I know I
never said to Harriet
(looking at her from my bed),

"Forget the damn thing—
I'd rather not have anything
between us."

Scott Lowe

Night Wind

There are places that only
The night wind knows,
Rushing black into arroyos
And mountain slopes that twist and curl
On the skirt of night.

The night wind caresses mesquite and creosote,
Moaning in her wooded throat a rhythmic rustle,
Sensual and private,
Where it is suddenly still
And a silhouette of stone
Stands sentinel.

GENERATIONS

The Bioillogical Blues

Cripes, it's not us, you know; it's only
Chemicals, synapses and hormones.
It's sullen or silent voices, compacts
Dropping, awkward telephones.

Yeah, you just got the tight skin
Socks and the mean red shoes:
You got a new case, baby,
Of the bioillogical blues.

AURIEL YOST

Research

Just as the price of pork bellies and
sorghum once consumed his thoughts,
the state of my health now
takes hold of his imagination.
Reference list in hand, he
haunts libraries, scours medical journals,
papers our bedroom with printouts of
protein cells, osteoblasts, osteoclasts.

Should the cricket-like click of
my vertebra or the snap
of a rib as I slip off my gown
bring me to his attention,
he might, just for a moment,
glance my way, before returning
to the text he lightly traces
with his index finger.

GENERATIONS

My Hair

My hair is falling out.
Stray hairs cling to the flannel
sheets on my hospital bed,
tangled strands litter the pillow.
I phone you, weep about my loss.
You tell me you love me,
that I should collect my hair.
you will braid it into a bracelet
for me to wear when I am well.
I spend the next few minutes
gingerly pulling hair from my head.
The roots slide from my scalp
as if embedded in butter.
When you visit I hand you the
hair sealed in a yellow envelope.
I watch from my window
after you leave, see you cross
the lawn to the parking lot and,
without breaking stride,
toss the envelope into a trash can.

WOJCIECH ZALEWSKI

Wojciech Zalewski

Creating

I always
wanted to build:
a pigeonhouse
because pigeons love forever;
an umbrella
protecting against mud;
soul
complacent toward my weaknesses;
mind
supposedly Wisdom created the world.

My hands
hatched small monsters while
the Tower of Babel
was still under construction,
languages already mixed.

Today
the joy of creativity
lingers despite
the reasons faded.

GENERATIONS

Slaves

Do not be afraid:
You will always have slaves
among you.
But give them freedom:
They will be grateful;
they will not curse;
they will give you a feeling of justice;
they will work for your life.
So, do not take from them
their meager goods.

Wojciech Zalewski

Suicide

Strive,
run to the curve of desire
where friend/enemy Death
awaits.

Ulysses' Sirens,
perhaps it is sweet
to die in your embraces,
break the mast,
rupture the bonds of convention.

You woo
like downing fog
whether over meadow
or over marsh,
by boots or boats,
transcended or succumbed,
charmed or stifled...

and the friend/enemy
giggles.

GENERATIONS

Homeless

Homeless brother,
do not lie on the city street,
for you make me feel either
guilty or cynical,
and either sensation
kills.

DAVID HARR

David Harr

Old Stale Yeast

Last night I uncapped my pen, and
I tapped into a priceless oil well...
At least I thought I had
Until my instructor got hold of my work...
It came back to me with more
Red ink than black.

FORCE THE READER TO MAKE THE LEAP
YOU'VE GOT TO FORCE THE READER TO
MAKE THE LEAP!
I wanted to force her to make the leap...
Only I was thinking more in terms of
The Grand Canyon

AND WHAT'S THIS INCESSANT
INFATUATION WITH RHYME?
I DON'T REMEMBER YOUR LAST NAME'S BEING
FROST
YOU'RE DESTROYING THE MOOD WITH THAT PUN
YOU MUST REMAIN CONSISTENT

As she shapes me and molds me with her
Enormous red pen...

I remain disobedient

GENERATIONS

Telegram to Nowhere

RARELY YOU WRITE
OR RETURN MY CALL

NOW WHO'LL CAST A LINE
WHEN I SLIP AND FALL

I'M TIRED OF WRITING
TO A BRICK WALL

DORA KUSHNER

Dora Kushner

Eruptions

When Joe and I visited Pompeii,
Sulphur dioxide fumes
Disintegrated my nylon stockings.
I could feel the gentle rivulets of threads
Trickle down my legs
Like the caresses of a lover.

When the second great San Francisco earthquake struck,
I felt gentle tremors in Yosemite.
Chandeliers swayed at the Ahwahnee.
Guests, bewildered, tried to call home.
Assured, we continued to enjoy nature.

Today papers, radio, T.V. announce:
"The Berlin Wall Has Come Down."
Bedlam...
The usual well-organized East Germans... Helpless!
Well-dressed young people with children,
Fleeing to West Germany like lemmings.
The crumbled wall has opened a can of worms

Old wounds reopened.
Caesar's mob has stormed the bastions.
Twenty-eight years of anger—vented
On the Wall:
Hammers, pickaxes,"Down! Down!" the cheers.

The unleashed energy comes
Tumbling forward...
Overflowing like lava
From Mt. Vesuvius.
Will it inundate the dictators?
And then, too,
What will survive?

Personal Values: Painting by Magritte

Somber, stark, stripped chamber
Speaks of grander days.
Beveled mirrored doors on the once-proud armoire
Reflect the image of a vain man.
Musty closet–worn garments
Carefully preserved...
Oversized bone comb and shaving brush
Trimmed with ebony and silver
Reveal bygone splendors.

No visible feminine baubles here,
In spite of the white–sheeted
Two–pillowed double bed.

Cirrocumulus clouds
Pervade the room
Forecasting a mighty marital rift.

Dora Kushner

Beware False Gods

Foolish sisters!
You've discovered false gods:
Commerce, Finance, Computers.
A cold, calculating world,
A new enslavement!

Confused sisters!
Use your new–found voices for liberty,
Freedom to sing a new song
Never sung before!

GENERATIONS

Springtime in Bruges—1520

Winter snows, spring rains
Revitalize and purify the sluggish waterways.

Venice of the North,
Romanticized, malodorous canals
Host stodgy young Flemish lovers.

Graceful swans on shore and water
Chaperone and guide the floating gondola,
Beaks pointing at the four doleful lovers
Ready to perform the rites of spring.

Cumulus clouds on the landscape
Portend a turbulent future.

On shore...
Galloping horsemen,
Spirited, rebellious, ready to pluck at life
Quickly, fearless and joyful...

While
The innocent lovers
Dutifully execute the mating ceremony,
Trapped by music, song, gondola, water.

The horsemen laugh, carouse.
If only momentarily, laugh they do!

ESTHER KAMKAR

Esther Kamkar

Hands in Tehran

My dark stained small hands
that peeled fresh walnut,
saved the white flesh
for marble pyramids,
have since whitened
in their longing
for a cherry tree
to climb.

I look back at the roads
cluttered with broken pyramids,
dried nails of dahlia petals,
*and crushed earrings of cherries.**

Afraid of becoming robed
in black like a crow
with the fingers and face of a woman,
How can I go home?

---

* A guote from Iranian woman poet Forough
Farokhzad.—E.K.

GENERATIONS

Connections

I. My Mother

When I called
to tell you that
Daniel was born,
when we cried together,
I felt like the longest
bridge over thirteen thousand
miles, connecting my first born
to my mother,
whose first born
had died
forty years before.

II. My Aunt

My Aunt Lady
who rode on horseback
from village to village
to deliver babies
was old with swollen legs
when I went to pay my respect.
She said
a woman should marry
before too long,
while her flesh is still edible.

III. My Grandmother

I remember
your white braids
colored at the ends
with deep red henna.

I remember
the golden moons
of your earrings.

I remember you
reading our lips
with the wisdom of
your hundred years.

I remember you
healing your broken old bones
with the power of your will
when you were hit by a car
while bringing bread to the poor.

I remember you
loving my name,
the same as a great aunt
and a distant queen.

GENERATIONS

IV. My Good Aunt

Her flower was
honeysuckle,
she was childless.

She gave me
a ruby hill
of pomegranate seeds
in a blue bowl.

VASSAR W. SMITH

Vassar W. Smith

Parcæ

The Fates will find a way to spoil the fun
   For us, if we will just live long enough:
We're only men, when all is said and done.

We think that we can overcome, outrun
   All consequences; time will call the bluff:
The Fates will find a way to spoil the fun.

. However thick or intricately spun
   The fiber, Atropos will cut and slough:
We're only men, when all is said and done.

Pleasure, in time, will pale for everyone:
   The wine turns rancid and the meat grows tough.
The Fates will find a way to spoil the fun.

Though some they grant a daughter or a son,
   Mortality remains: no getting off.
We're only men when all is said and done.

What lies beyond, who knows? We may go on
   To heroes' peace. Here, mired in mortal stuff,
The Fates will find a way to spoil the fun:
We're only men when all is said and done.

GENERATIONS

Tema con Variazioni

My pride is dust! I'll never learn the way.
Much truth, alas, is lost upon the hearer.
Since intercourse requires a bit of play,
She shakes her ass in front of Grandma's mirror.

My pride is dust! I'll never learn the way:
Since intercourse is lost upon the hearer,
She shakes her ass, requires a bit of play,
Much truth, alas, in front of Grandma's mirror!

Much truth, alas, is lost upon the hearer.
She shakes her ass,— I'll never learn the way!
Since intercourse in front of Grandma's mirror
My pride is dust, requires a bit of play.

Since intercourse requires a bit of play,
My pride is dust in front of Grandma's mirror.
Much truth, alas, I'll never learn: The way
She shakes her ass is lost upon the hearer.

She shakes her ass in front of Grandma's mirror!
Much truth, alas, requires a bit of play.
"My pride is dust!" is lost upon the hearer...
Since intercourse I'll never learn the way!

Since intercourse requires a bit of play,
Much truth, alas, is lost upon the hearer.
My pride is dust! I'll never learn, the way
She shakes her ass in front of Grandma's mirror!

Vassar W. Smith

Two Men in White

He sat at a table in Philadelphia,
In a white dinner jacket a large, fat man
With red wine and a plate of spaghetti and meatballs.
He'd hit the heights, then hit the skids.
Now, they said he was making a comeback.
He'd played the role but knew in his heart
He'd never be another Caruso.
He'd had his chance and let it slip:
He'd drunk too much and wouldn't practice.
Now there were whispers, reproach and pity,
When people looked at the large, fat man,
Making a comeback that no one believed in.

When he could bear these whispers no longer,
Right there in the midst of the party
He lifted the plate of spaghetti and meatballs
And turned it over upon his head,
Spilling the food all over himself,
Pouring red sauce on his fine while suit.
Some gasped, some laughed, but all these sounds
Were just as instantly cut short
When the fat man opened his mouth—and sang:
Puccini's notes rang in their ears,
All present thoughts were snatched away,
And, if for only that one moment,
Everyone who heard that voice
Saw only Pinkerton with Butterfly.

And, just as suddenly, when the voice
Stopped singing, the people again saw only
A fat man, an overturned plate on his head,
And a white suit covered with spaghetti and meatballs.
And just in case the point was lost
On anybody at his party,
Lanza told his speechless guests
Before he rose and left the room:
"La voce, la voce... la voce è tutto!"
("The voice, the voice... The voice is everything!")

GENERATIONS

Three thousand miles and half a lifetime
Beyond this, why do I find myself
Again reflecting on Mario Lanza?
I guess, because I see another
Man in white, though neither large
Nor fat, nor formally attired.
I see a slim, gray-bearded man
Too old to show himself in public
In a T-shirt, jeans and tennis shoes.
I see a man whose poems on paper
Show no grasp of poetic form
Nor sense in any way engaging.
They all sing the same song of self:
How much he loves or aches or longs,
Or, worse, describe his body parts
And all that's right or wrong with his sex–life.

Whatever else it isn't poetry
That he purveys: it reads like prose—
But oh, the voice that he has learned
To orchestrate such common words
When reading what he calls a poem!
Oh, the melodious baritone!
Oh, the too-clear enunciation!
Worst of all, the illusory sympathy
As though he were speaking to every listener
Personally. But somehow I doubt
That he could listen to others' words
As he expects his own to be heard.

Such is our age, that "kiss and tell"
Can be confused with poetry; but even—
Or especially—in such an age,
When knowledge, logic, form are optional,
"La voce, la voce… la voce è tutto!"

ANATOLE LUBOVICH

GENERATIONS

«Ну, целуй меня, целуй,...»

Ну, целуй меня, целуй,
Хоть до крови, хоть до боли.
Не в ладу с холодной волей
Кипяток сердечных струй.

Опрокинутая кружка
Средь веселых не для нас.
Понимай меня подружка,
На земле живут лишь раз!

Оглядись спокойным взором,
Посмотри: во мгле сырой
Месяц, словно желтый ворон,
Кружит, вьется над землей.

Ну, целуй же. Так хочу я.
Песню тлен пропел и мне.
Видно смерть мою почуял
Тот, кто вьется в вышине.

Увядающая сила!
Умирать—так умирать!
До кончины губы милой
Я хотел бы целовать.

Чтоб все время в синих дремах,
Не стыдясь и не тая,
В нежном шелесте черемух
Раздавалось: «Я твое».

И чтоб свет на полной кружке
Легкой пеной не погас—
Пей и пой, моя подружка:
На земле живут лишь раз!

— Сергей Есенин

"Kiss me with a kiss beblooded,…"
By Sergei Yesenin
Translated by Anatole Lubovich

Kiss me with a kiss beblooded,
Kiss me with a kiss of pain,
Frigid freedom is not suited
For my heartflow's boiling drain.

Merrymakers' tumbled tankard
Is no longer meant for us.
Understand, my friend and sweetheart,
Life on earth but once will pass.

In the humid haze of heaven
You can see it, turn around:
Moon, as if a yellow raven,
Spins and circles over ground.

Kiss me, then! It's what I'm craving.
I can hear the tune of rot.
He, who whirls around in heaven,
Senses, seems, my death-bound lot.

Hear me, o you force of wither,
If to die, I would die well!
Dearest darling, I would kiss her
On the lips of last farewell.

So that in the blue of slumber,
Where nor shame nor passion rules,
Gentle rustle of the bramble
Would but whisper,"I am yours."

Lest the light on brimful tankard
Fade to frothy nothingness,
Drink and sing, my friend and sweetheart:
Life on earth but once will pass

FOR THE HOLIDAY SEASON

Advent

Christmas is coming!
I hear it singing
in the wind chimes over the deck.
There's a waiting stillness
to the dried corn stalks.
The yellow whir of cedar waxwings
scatters pyrocantha berries
over the frozen lipia berries. One year

when I was small,
I took Christmas cookies
to the poor family down the hill.
Eerie tree forms skulked through the dense fog
and the air rang
with the voices of caroling robins
hidden in its heavy shroud.
Over my head madrones shook,
raining their crimson fruit—
a multitude of fluttering wings!—
and I was sure the angels had arrived.

Today in the gray mist
white dahlia heads loom
in the garden like ghost lanterns.
Venus has taken vigil in the west.
The world once more in breathless hope
awaits the Great Event.

— **Carol Hankermeyer**

GENERATIONS

"Ribbons and evergreens..."

Ribbons and evergreens, candles and bells,
And most of all You
Lord Jesus the Christ,
Born on earth that we on earth
May learn to live in love and peace
With God, each other, and ourselves,
And with the earth itself
And all that comes from it.

Ribbons and evergreens, candles and bells,
And, above all, the Spirit that calls to all:
To remember the hungry and feed them;
To remember the homeless and give them shelter;
To remember the abused and stop the abuse;
To remember the lonely and embrace them
In our lives and hearts, not only in our arms;
And to treasure and protect
The life, health and joy of every child
As we would treasure and protect
That child at Bethlehem.

Ribbons and evergreens, candles and bells,
Carols and feasts delight the senses.
The heart must know, however,
That all hinges on one great If/Then.

For:

If
If You
If You, Jesus,
If You, Jesus, weren't
If You, Jesus, weren't born
If You, Jesus, weren't born in
If You, Jesus, weren't born in me
If You, Jesus, weren't born in me and
If You, Jesus, weren't born in me and this
If You, Jesus, weren't born in me and this world,

Then,

This season and all this life
Would hold nothing better than
Ribbons and evergreens, candles and bells.

—Vassar W. Smith

GENERATIONS

Wait, O Wise Men *

Wait, o wise men, eastern monarchs,
What's your urgent hurry?
What's this star that now above us
Shines in brilliant glory?
   What can the newborn Child reveal that's
   Worthy of your hardship?
   Can these strange reports be real that
   Summon you to worship?

This new Infant whom you'll find is
Resting in a manger,
While King Herod's jealous mind is
Casting Him in danger.
   Surely to perceive you're able
   That this King of lepers
   For a palace has a stable
   And its court of shepherds.

Why should such a lowly Being
Draw you from a far land?
For His Crown mankind is weaving
Him a thorny garland.
   Now in Mary's lap He's resting,
   But what of tomorrow?
   Life of pain and scorn await Him,
   Full of pain and sorrow.

"We have come compelled by ancient
Prophecy's persuasion.
Love and peace this son of transients
Brings to every nation.
   Not in wealth of worldly measure
   Is His realm's foundation,
   But in hearts of all who treasure
   Gift of His salvation."

                    —Tomás San Andreas

---

* Adapted from an Eastern European Christmas carol.

READERS' RESPONSE TO

The Clock, Desperados, and Jeremy: The 1992 Zapizdat Anthology

The sky isn't falling, but I think a piece of it, in the form of this book, just hit me on the head,- one true test of a collection of great poetry (or at least an anthology with no *bad* poems in it). Too often these days, poets — whether aspiring or acknowledged — only put readers to sleep. Not here! Thank you, editor Basil Meyerhold and all the fine poets between the covers for waking me with this poetry.

Kevin Arnold, the first of the featured poets, instantly grabs and holds the reader's attention. His poem "Nightcap" hits home, hard, like a knockout punch from a world heavyweight boxing champ.

The poems of **Sally Croft** present some painfully beautiful insights. Especially tantalizing are her companion poems "Dürer's Adam" and "Dürer's Eve." Adam is bewildered at his Eve-induced arousal; Eve is fascinated, not by her mate, but by the subtle symmetry of the serpent.

Wojciech Zalewski, in his poem "The Clock" offers a fine piece of whimsy, in the vein of J. M. Barrie's prose: time passes, leaving us lonely for not responding to the knocks on our doors that we failed to heed.

The collection also includes a generous helping of humor. **S. V. Williams** parodies four famous lyrics of A. E. Housman. The fourth ("Oh, who is that poor sinner?") conjures up a devastatingly funny vision of a recent celebrity's sensational legal ordeal. In "Felis Parasiticus" **Vassar W. Smith** pokes fun at the common house-cat:"Down-and-out aristocrat, saved from kitty-jail, / You're a five-dollar cat with a hundred-dollar tail!"

Jeanne C. Watson concludes this anthology with her poem "In Praise of Men." It is high time that contemporary poets recognized and praised the vulnerability of true maleness. Ms. Watson has done a superb job.

When we are young, we have our dreams; when we are old, our memories of youth sustain us. *The Clock, Desperados, and Jeremy* passes this critic's reality check and goes on to attain a "must read" rating: on a four-point scale, it merits all four stars. - ****

— **Beecher Smith**

The Clock, Desperados, and Jeremy:
The 1992 Zapizdat Anthology
Ed. Basil Meyerhold
(Zapizdat Publications, 112 pages)

There is a marked difference between run-of-the-mill magazine poems and many of the poems in a collection beguilingly titled The *Clock, Desperados, and Jeremy.* This anthology, issued from the almost as beguilingly named Zapizdat Publications of Palo Alto, dares to be irregular in its disregard for pale likeness. Much lively wit is displayed. Few poems are self-consciously, modishly grim or grimly sentimental; some express oddity without strain. The run of poems in this collection should be considered playful in the best sense.Some poets, especially the featured Kevin Arnold and Sally Croft, are notably sure of their formal procedures; Another rarity here is a group of poems in both English and Polish by Wojciech Zalewski, author of two collections published in Poland. Translating his own poems and making others in English, Zalewski has achieved his special niche.

But the whole anthology is itself singular in the comparative dearth of trivial autobiographical anecdotes, staples of the so-called postmodern phase of composition..S. V. Williams ' parodies of Housman, his carefree "Metamorphosis" (about a grasshopper "of Texan dimensions" achieving mythic identity), his ridiculing of someone's pretentious diction all mark him as an experienced satirist. Succeeding pieces by Vassar Smith possess a comparable command of form and language.Smith's pieces begin in a light-verse vain, but his poem of tribute to his mother shows a mastery of an open form. The anthology concludes with the thought-provoking poems of J. C. Watson. Particularly fine is her "Pittsburgh, City of Fire." Offered as "The 1992 Zapizdat Anthology," this collection prods the reader to look beyond 1992 for more such refreshing contributions from the intriguing, Slavic-sounding Zapizdat press.

—Richard Clemente

"Thanks for... *The Clock, Desperados, and Jeremy.* There are a lot of good poems in it. It's a worthy poetry book, which is pretty uncommon."

— Simeon Stylites, Feh! Press, New York

THE CLOCK, DESPERADOS AND JEREMY: THE 1992 ZAPIZDAT ANTHOLOGY. Fine poetry by Kevin Arnold, Sally Croft, Wojciech Zalewski et al. Ed. Basil Meyerhold. 112 pp.

$5.95   ISBN 1–880964–03–1

INTO THE LIMERICK GROVE: 156 ORIGINAL LIMERICKS BY CONTEMPORARY AUTHORS. Rib–racking amusement from limerick masters Laurence Perrine, Arthur Deex, Vassar Smith, Ann Gasser et al. 112 pp.

$6.95   ISBN 1–880964–04-X

THE OVEN–BIRD CHORUS: POEMS. By Vassar W. Smith and S. V. Williams. 40 pp.

$5.95   ISBN 1–880964–05–8